I0797909

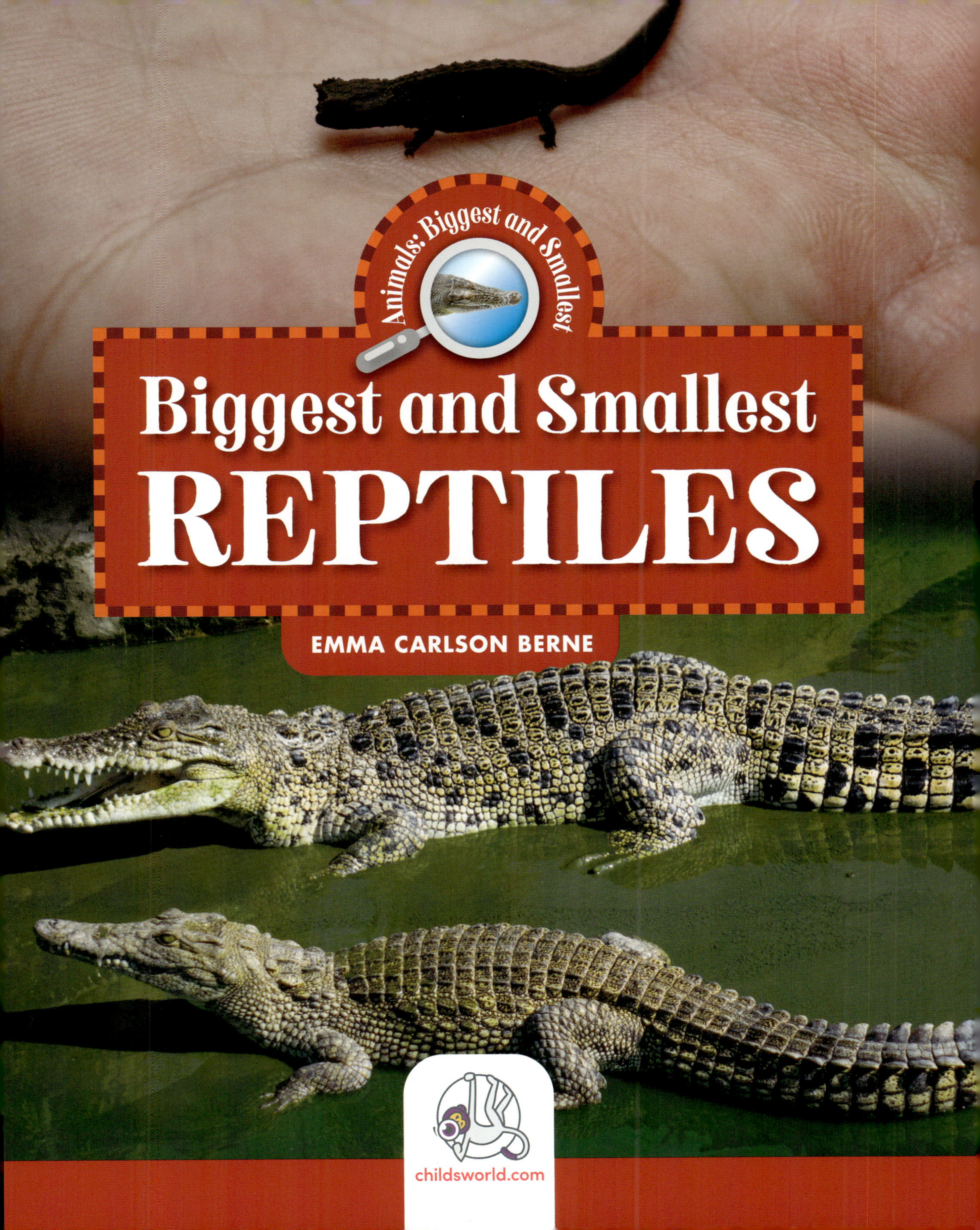
Animals: Biggest and Smallest
Biggest and Smallest
REPTILES
EMMA CARLSON BERNE
childsworld.com

Published by The Child's World®
800-599-READ • childsworld.com

Photography Credits
Cover: ©chriscasey/Shutterstock; ©Uckarintra Wongcharit/Shutterstock; ©Cobalt S-Elinoi/Shutterstock; ©Madelein_Wolf/iStock/Getty Images; page 2: ©Artush/iStock/Getty Images; page 3: ©dwi putra stock/Shutterstock; page 3: ©Madelein_Wolf/iStock/Getty Images; page 5: ©Roberto Dani/Shutterstock; page 5: ©Glaw, F., Köhler, J., Hawlitschek, O. et al. Extreme miniaturization of a new amniote vertebrate and insights into the evolution of genital size in chameleons. Sci Rep 11, 2522 (2021). https://doi.org/10.1038/s41598-020-80955-1/Wikimedia Commons; page 6–7: ©Rizky Ade Jonathan/Shutterstock; page 8–9: ©Nick Brundle Photography/Moment/Getty Images; page 9: ©Supermop/Shutterstock; page 10–11: ©Wolfgang Kaehler/LightRocket/Getty Images; page 12–13, 21: ©Wolfgang Kaehler/LightRocket/Getty Images; page 14–15: ©VectorSilhouettes/iStock/Getty Images; page 15: ©Leontura/DigitalVision Vectors/Getty Images; page 15: ©sabelskaya/iStock/Getty Images; page 16: ©Satab Gnana/Shutterstock; page 16–17: ©Sazid Rezwan/Shutterstock; page 19, 21: ©Danny Ye/Shutterstock; page 19: ©Wolfgang Kaehler/LightRocket/Getty Images; page 20: ©Cobalt S-Elinoi/Shutterstock; page 22: ©Kozak Sergii/Shutterstock; page 22: ©masa44/Shutterstock; page 22: ©New Africa/Shutterstock.

ISBN Information
9781503875654 (Reinforced Library Binding)
9781503876170 (Portable Document Format)
9781503876798 (Online Multi-user eBook)
9781503877290 (Electronic Publication)

LCCN
2025938252

Printed in the United States of America

ABOUT THE AUTHOR

Emma Carlson Berne often writes about nature and animals, especially for young readers. She loves exploring the natural world in her free time as well. Emma lives in Cincinnati with her husband, three sons, one grumpy cat, and one friendly cat.

Table of Contents

Big and Little

A tiny **chameleon** skitters through leaves on the forest floor. *Brookesia nana* is the world's smallest **reptile**. It is commonly known as the nano-chameleon. It can perch on the tip of your finger. Now, zip over to a river on the coast of Australia. A giant saltwater crocodile is lurking in the water. As the biggest reptile in the world, it can easily snatch a deer that comes to drink.

Animals' sizes help them exist in their surroundings. Big animals, such as the saltwater crocodile, can hunt a wide variety of **prey**. They might have fewer **predators**. Small animals, including the nano-chameleon, can hide from predators in tiny spaces. Big or small, animals are perfectly **adapted** to their **habitats**.

Many reptiles, including saltwater crocodiles, blend in with their surroundings.

The smallest reptile on Earth fits easily on the end of a person's finger!

Where Do Saltwater Crocodiles Live?

Arctic Ocean

North America

Europe

Asia

Atlantic Ocean

Pacific Ocean

Africa

Pacific Ocean

South America

Indian Ocean

Australia

KEY

Saltwater Crocodile Range

Saltwater crocodiles usually only come out of the water to warm up in the sun.

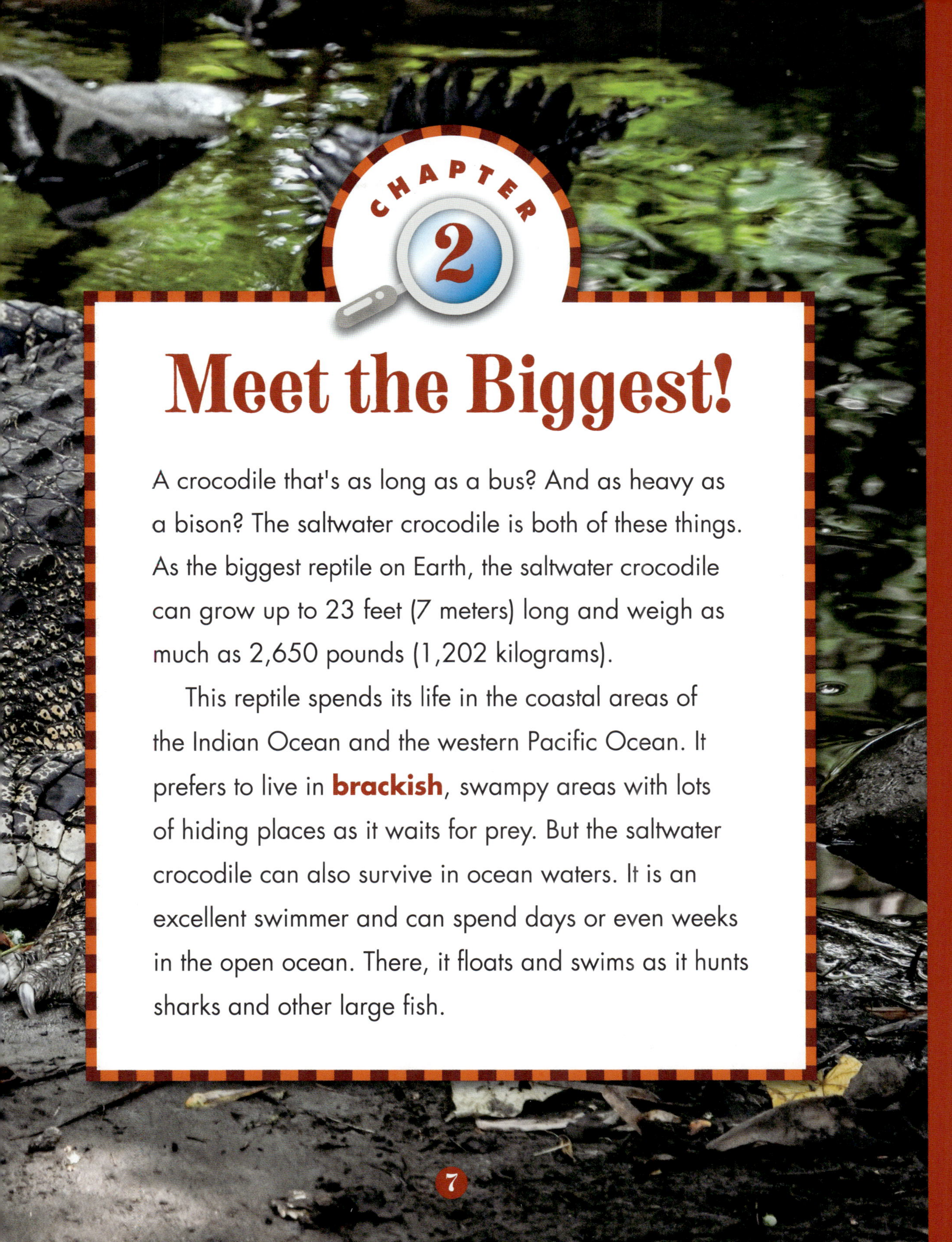

CHAPTER 2

Meet the Biggest!

A crocodile that's as long as a bus? And as heavy as a bison? The saltwater crocodile is both of these things. As the biggest reptile on Earth, the saltwater crocodile can grow up to 23 feet (7 meters) long and weigh as much as 2,650 pounds (1,202 kilograms).

This reptile spends its life in the coastal areas of the Indian Ocean and the western Pacific Ocean. It prefers to live in **brackish**, swampy areas with lots of hiding places as it waits for prey. But the saltwater crocodile can also survive in ocean waters. It is an excellent swimmer and can spend days or even weeks in the open ocean. There, it floats and swims as it hunts sharks and other large fish.

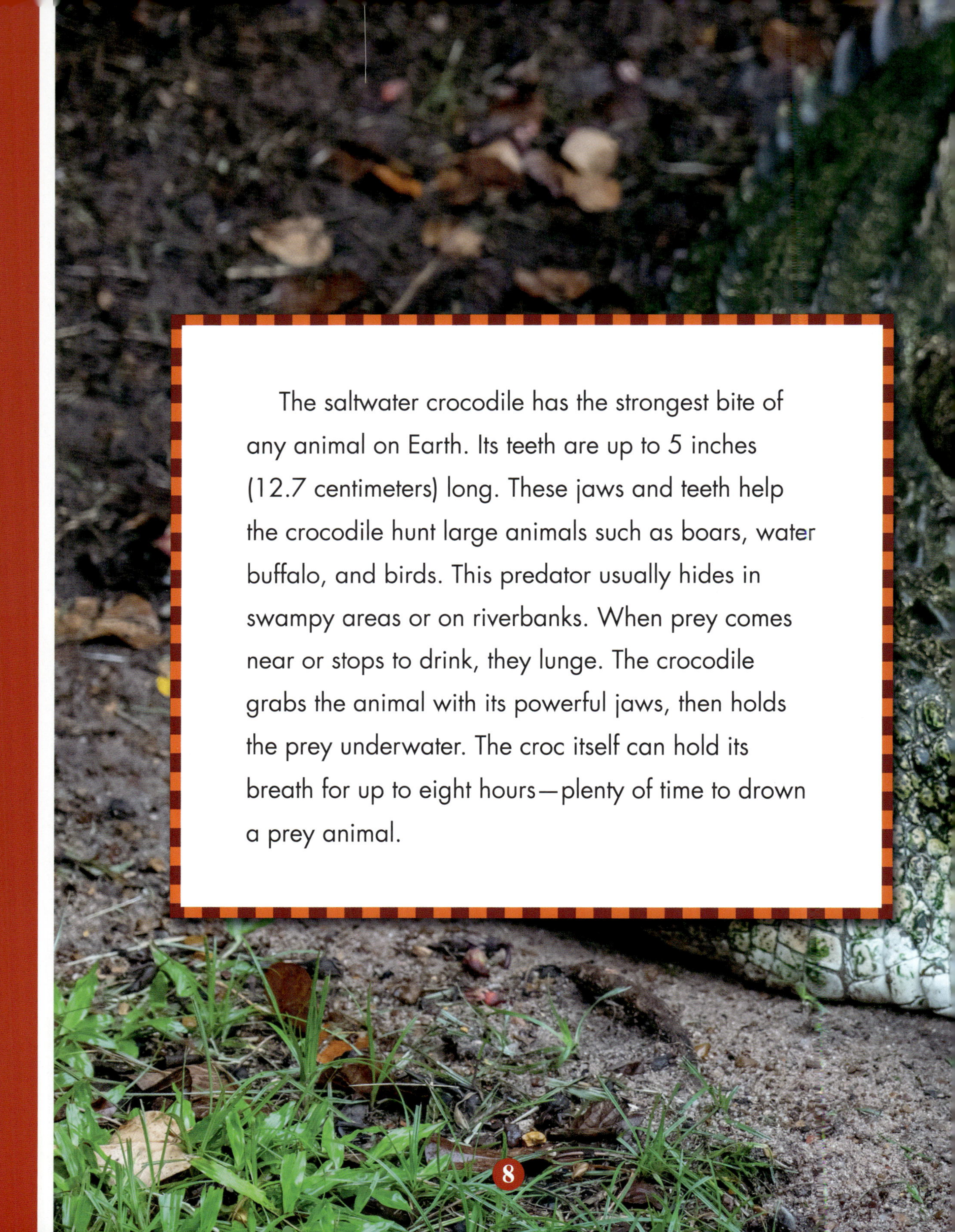

The saltwater crocodile has the strongest bite of any animal on Earth. Its teeth are up to 5 inches (12.7 centimeters) long. These jaws and teeth help the crocodile hunt large animals such as boars, water buffalo, and birds. This predator usually hides in swampy areas or on riverbanks. When prey comes near or stops to drink, they lunge. The crocodile grabs the animal with its powerful jaws, then holds the prey underwater. The croc itself can hold its breath for up to eight hours—plenty of time to drown a prey animal.

SALTWATER CROCODILE MOTHERS AND BABIES

Saltwater crocodiles are careful mothers. They build nests of sticks and grass along riverbanks or other dry spots near water. There, they lay about 50 eggs. The mother crocodile guards her nest fiercely while the eggs are developing. Then, when the baby crocodiles hatch, the mother carries them in her mouth or on her back down to a safe spot in the water. She stays with her babies to protect them for about five weeks before finally leaving them to make their own way.

Saltwater crocodiles have around 66 teeth.

Where Do Nano-Chameleons Live?

Nano-chameleons have shorter tails than their larger relatives.

Meet the Smallest!

In 2021, scientists in the Madagascar rainforests got a big—or actually a very *tiny*—surprise. They found a chameleon the size of a sunflower seed under the leaves on the forest floor. This tiny reptile was only about 0.6 inches (15.2 millimeters) long.

Eventually, the scientists named this lizard *Brookesia nana*, or "nano-chameleon." The male in the **species** is the smallest of all the 11,500 known reptile species on Earth. Other lizards are *almost* as tiny. The female Jaragua dwarf gecko measures about 0.6 to 0.7 inches (15.2 to 17.8 mm), and the Virgin Islands dwarf gecko is also only 0.7 inches (17.8 mm). But the nano-chameleon holds the record—so far!

These tiny chameleons stay close to the forest floor. They live on fallen leaves and among moss and grass.

The nano-chameleon spends its life on the forest floor where it hunts an equally tiny prey—**mites**. It can hide from predators in a blade of grass. In fact, the nano-chameleon has lots of company in its Madagascar rainforest habitat. This island nation is home to around 100 other species of chameleon.

But the nano-chameleon and the other lizards of Madagascar are far from safe. The forests that they depend upon for survival are under threat from **deforestation**. As trees are cut for logging or to clear for farming, the forest floor that shelters the nano-chameleon is cleared as well.

How They Compare

Saltwater crocodiles and the nano-chameleon certainly appear to be very different reptiles. After all, one is half as long as a bus and one can fit comfortably on a nickel! The saltwater crocodile is as heavy as a large horse, but the nano-chameleon weighs about as much as a paper clip. But the Earth's biggest and smallest reptiles are both predators. Their prey matches their size, with saltwater crocodiles hunting bigger animals and the nano-chameleon hunting tiny mites and insects.

MEASURING UP

You probably won't run into a saltwater crocodile or a nano-chameleon on a walk in your neighborhood. But even if you did, you probably wouldn't notice either of them. They are both good at hiding—one because of its tiny size, and the other because it likes to hide just below the water's surface. Even the biggest of reptiles can stay out of sight!

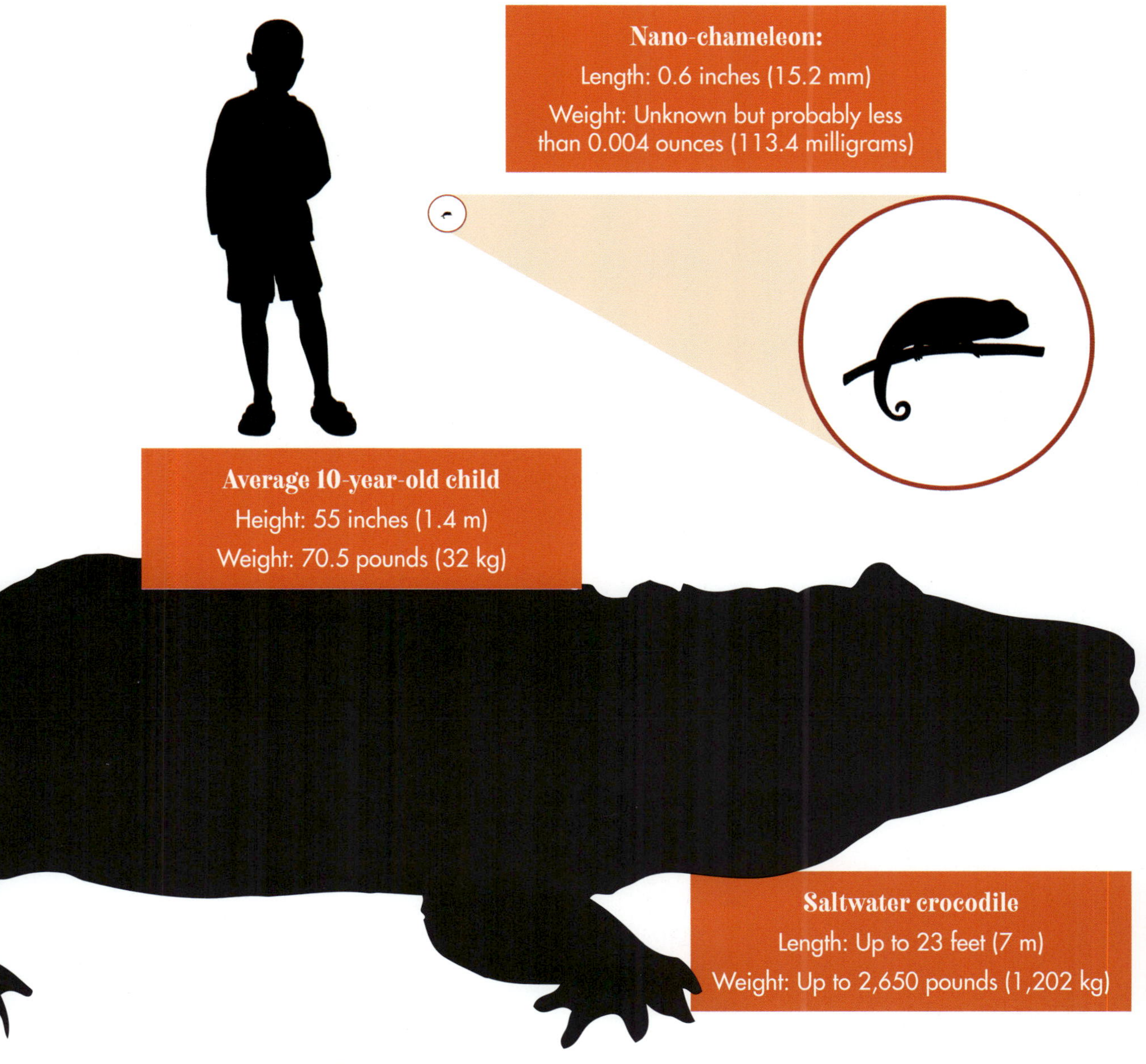

CHAMELEON CAMOUFLAGE

The little brown nano-chameleon cannot change color, unlike many of its fellow chameleons. Chameleons usually climb around in trees. Changing color from brown to green and back again helps them blend in. But the nano-chameleon doesn't need this survival strategy. It lives only on the forest floor, where brown is the only necessary **camouflage** color.

Saltwater crocodiles prefer to spend most of their time in the water.

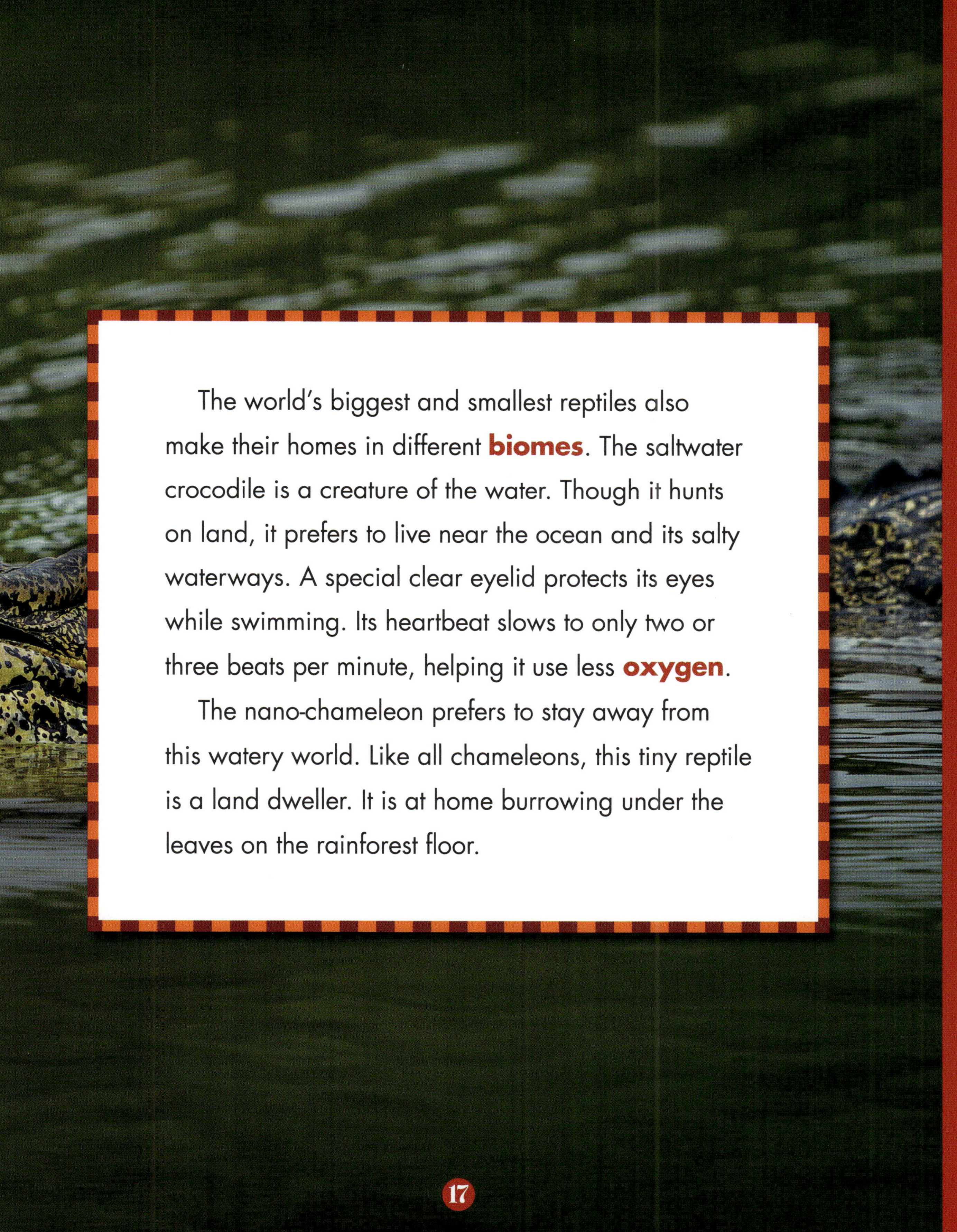

The world's biggest and smallest reptiles also make their homes in different **biomes**. The saltwater crocodile is a creature of the water. Though it hunts on land, it prefers to live near the ocean and its salty waterways. A special clear eyelid protects its eyes while swimming. Its heartbeat slows to only two or three beats per minute, helping it use less **oxygen**.

The nano-chameleon prefers to stay away from this watery world. Like all chameleons, this tiny reptile is a land dweller. It is at home burrowing under the leaves on the rainforest floor.

Survival Strategies

Crocs and chameleons have to work to stay alive! Protecting themselves against predators is key. The saltwater crocodile is lucky—it has almost no known predators. In fact, humans and habitat loss kill more crocodiles than anything else. But the nano-chameleon has a different story. This tiny chameleon is preyed upon by snakes, birds, monkeys, and other mammals. Insects such as ants can eat their eggs. Still, the nano-chameleon has some survival strategies of its own. This mini-reptile is excellent at hiding in tiny spots a predator might not be able to reach. It can also dart away quickly when danger in the form of a beak or a mouth comes near!

Saltwater crocodiles prefer to stay away from humans.

People often try to capture nano-chameleons and keep them for pets.

One World, Big and Small

One reptile eats mites. One reptile eats water buffalo. One can tuck itself into a folded blade of grass. Another can swim for days in the open ocean. Yet these two animals are both members of the diverse world of reptiles. And their very different habitats are both in danger from the effects of rising temperatures on Earth, deforestation, and agriculture. Protecting these animals, and the places they live, is a simple, similar goal all humans can work toward.

WONDER MORE

Wondering About New Information:

What did you learn about saltwater crocodiles and nano-chameleons? Write down three new facts you learned. Did this information surprise you? Why or why not?

Wondering How It Matters:

The nano-chameleon's rainforest home is under threat. Why is it important to learn about animal habitats?

Wondering Why:

Why does the nano-chameleon lack the ability to change color? Do you think that's a good thing? Explain your answer.

Ways to Keep Wondering:

After reading this book, what questions do you still have about saltwater crocodiles and nano-chameleons? What can you do to learn more about them?

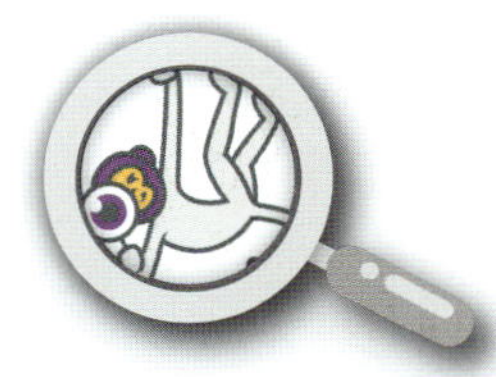

MAKE A CROCODILE HAND PUPPET

Supplies

- a brown paper lunch sack
- scissors
- glue
- green and white construction paper
- a black and a green marker

Make your own puppet—with a bite! You can use simple supplies from around your house to create this sack craft.

Directions

1 Lay your bag out so that the end flap faces you. This will be the face and mouth of your crocodile.

2 Using your scissors, cut out about five to eight smal triangles from your white construction paper. These are your crocodile teeth.

3 Glue the teeth just underneath the flap of the paper bag so that they are visible when the flap is flat.

4 Now, cut out two small semicircles from your green construction paper.

5 Glue these to the back of the flap so that they stick up when the bag is flat. These are your crocodile eyes.

6 Color a black dot in the middle of the green, sticking-up eyes.

7 Using both your green and black markers, color a snout on the flap of the paper bag.

8 Then, stick your hand in the bag and bring your crocodile to life!

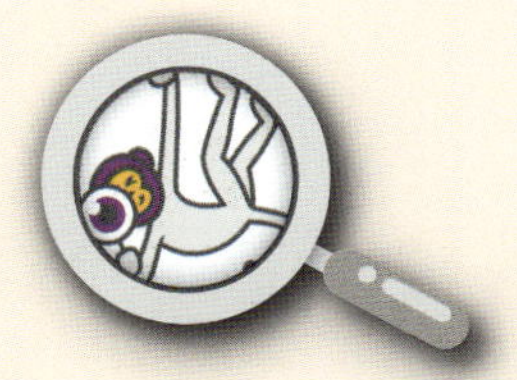

GLOSSARY

adapted (uh-DAP-ted) Animals that have adapted have changed to fit their environment.

biomes (BY-ohmz) Biomes are areas defined by the species that live in that location.

brackish (BRAK-ish) Brackish water is somewhat salty, but not as salty as the sea.

camouflage (KAH-muh-flazh) Camouflage helps animals disguise themselves to blend into their environment.

chameleon (kuh-MEE-lee-yun) A chameleon is a small lizard that can often change its color to its surroundings.

deforestation (dee-for-uhs-TAY-shun) Deforestation is the intentional clearing of forested land.

habitats (HA-buh-tats) Habitats are the places where animals live.

mites (MYTS) A mite is a type of tiny arachnid.

oxygen (OX-uh-jen) Oxygen is a colorless gas needed for life on Earth.

predators (PRE-duh-terz) Predators are animals that hunt other animals for food.

prey (PRAY) Prey are animals that are hunted and eaten by other animals.

reptile (REP-tyl) Reptiles are cold-blooded, scaly creatures with backbones that lay soft-shelled eggs.

species (SPEE-sheez) A species is a group of living things that are able to reproduce with each other.

FIND OUT MORE

In the Library

Maloney, Brenna. *Reptiles*. New York, NY: Scholastic, 2023.

Rathburn, Betsy. *Remarkable Reptiles*. Minnetonka, MN: Bellwether Media, 2023.

Reed, Ellis M. *Alligators and Crocodiles*. Parker, CO: The Child's World, 2020.

On the Web

Visit our website for links about the biggest and smallest reptiles:
childsworld.com/links

Note to Parents, Caregivers, Teachers, and Librarians: We routinely verify our web links to make sure they are safe and active sites. So encourage your readers to check them out!

INDEX